What's It Like Out?
Twister!

Kris Hirschmann

ABDO
Publishing Company

visit us at
www.abdopublishing.com

Published by ABDO Publishing Company, 8000 West 78th Street, Edina, Minnesota 55439.
Copyright © 2008 by Abdo Consulting Group, Inc. International copyrights reserved in all
countries. No part of this book may be reproduced in any form without written permission from the
publisher. The Checkerboard Library™ is a trademark and logo of ABDO Publishing Company.

Printed in the United States.

Cover Photo: iStockphoto
Interior Photos: AP Images pp. 17, 23, 27; Greg Henshall/FEMA p. 22; iStockphoto pp. 1, 4, 9, 10;
    National Geographic Image Collection p. 17; National Oceanic and Atmospheric
    Administration/Department of Commerce pp. 7, 13, 20, 25; Peter Arnold pp. 5, 8, 11, 16;
    Photo Researchers, Inc. pp. 14, 15, 29; Robert J. Alvey/FEMA p. 19; TSgt. Bill Kimble/U.S.
    Department of Defense p. 18; Visible Earth/NASA p. 21

Series Coordinator: Megan M. Gunderson
Editors: Megan M. Gunderson, BreAnn Rumsch
Art Direction & Cover Design: Neil Klinepier

Library of Congress Cataloging-in-Publication Data

Hirschmann, Kris, 1967-
  Twister! / Kris Hirschmann.
      p. cm. -- (What's it like out?)
  Includes bibliographical references and index.
  ISBN 978-1-59928-946-5
  1. Tornadoes--Juvenile literature. I. Title.

  QC955.2.H57 2008
  551.55'3--dc22
                                    2007029159

Contents

Twister!

Imagine you are looking out the window on a stormy afternoon. Dark clouds blanket the sky. Earlier, there was light rain. But now, heavier rain is falling, and hail is pelting your window. You also notice the sky has taken on a greenish tint.

"It's going to be a bad one," you think.

Just then, a bulge appears on the bottom of a distant cloud. It seems to grow downward. Meanwhile, you notice the clouds are spinning. You gasp and run for shelter. A tornado is heading your way!

Make sure you head for shelter when a storm is approaching!

Tornadoes are the most violent storms on Earth. They are sometimes called twisters. Witnessing a twister forming may be rare. Yet many tornadoes do touch down each year. When they do, they can harm homes, people, animals, forests, and anything else in their paths.

People say approaching tornadoes are so loud they sound like jet engines or freight trains.

Where Tornadoes Occur

Tornadoes occur all over the world. They have been seen on every continent except Antarctica. Tornadoes are most common in the United States, which reports about 1,000 of them per year. Tornadoes also affect Canada, the United Kingdom, Russia, Australia, Bangladesh, and many other countries.

Most U.S. tornadoes occur in an area nicknamed Tornado Alley. This region covers the southwestern **plains** of the United States. Within Tornado Alley, twisters are most common in Texas, Oklahoma, Kansas, and Nebraska. Iowa, Illinois, Indiana, Ohio, Wisconsin, Michigan, Minnesota, and Kentucky commonly experience tornadoes, too.

These storms plague Tornado Alley for a reason. Cold polar air and warm tropical air meet in this region. Unstable conditions occur when there is warm, moist air near the

surface and cool, dry air above it. Together, these conditions can cause storms. And sometimes, these storms create tornadoes.

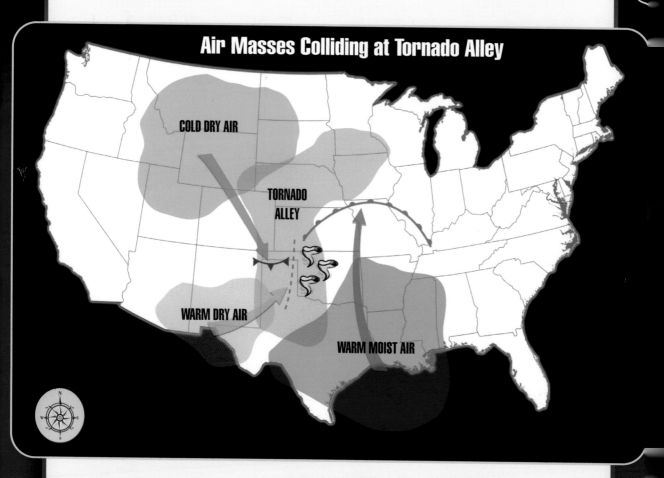

Air Masses Colliding at Tornado Alley

COLD DRY AIR

TORNADO ALLEY

WARM DRY AIR

WARM MOIST AIR

Tornado Season

Tornadoes have occurred on every day of the year. But tornado activity is greatest at certain times of the year, depending on the region. In late summer and early autumn, the temperature and moisture differences between polar and tropical **air masses** are smaller. Severe storms are less common in these conditions, so tornadoes form less often.

Tornado sirens warn people to seek shelter when a tornado has been spotted.

Tornado season shifts north and south depending on how far south the cold air reaches. When spring arrives, days grow longer and the land heats up. Tropical air moves in, pushing the cooler air northward. As the border between the two **air masses** moves across an area, tornadoes become more common there.

In the United States, the temperature and moisture differences are greater from April through June. So each year, hundreds of twisters appear during these months. Tornadoes are especially common in May.

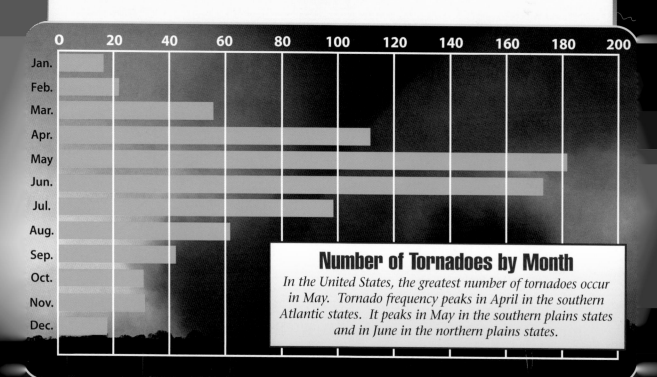

	0	20	40	60	80	100	120	140	160	180	200
Jan.											
Feb.											
Mar.											
Apr.											
May											
Jun.											
Jul.											
Aug.											
Sep.											
Oct.											
Nov.											
Dec.											

Number of Tornadoes by Month

In the United States, the greatest number of tornadoes occur in May. Tornado frequency peaks in April in the southern Atlantic states. It peaks in May in the southern plains states and in June in the northern plains states.

A Storm Forms

Unstable conditions occur because of air's weight. In warm air, tiny particles called molecules have a lot of energy. They zip around quickly and are far apart. Molecules in cold air have less energy. They move more slowly and are packed closer together. For this reason, cold air is **denser** than warm air. So, it puts more pressure on the things it touches.

Air pressure differences also cause the wind to blow.

Pressure differences always try to even themselves out. So when warm and cold **air masses** meet, the air starts to shift. Cold air may flow toward warm air in a windy stream. Or warm, moist air may

A cumulonimbus cloud may be 60,000 feet (18,000 m) tall!

bubble upward through a cool, dry layer. Either way, air is on the move. This is what scientists mean when they say the air is unstable.

Moving air does not always cause storms. But if lots of warm, moist air rises and cools, a towering cumulonimbus cloud may appear. More and more air rises into the growing cloud. These **updrafts** carry the warm, moist air that feeds the growing storm.

Tornado Conditions

An **updraft** is not the only moving air at work in a storm. Winds blow in different directions and at different speeds. These differences are called wind shear. **Vertical** direction shear refers to the change in direction with height. The increase in wind speed with height is called vertical speed shear.

Sometimes, wind shear makes the air tumble, like a log spinning on a river. At first, the tumbling air is **horizontal**. But soon, it gets caught in the cloud's central updraft. It tilts upward until it is vertical. This causes the updraft to rotate as it continues feeding the storm.

At this point, the entire center of the storm cloud is spinning slowly. The area of rotating, rising air is between 6 and 12 miles (10 and 20 km) wide. This is now called a mesocyclone (meh-zuh-SEYE-klohn).

Sometimes, the mesocyclone blasts air upward with great force. The air from this strong **updraft** then erupts through the cloud's **anvil**-shaped top. When it does, a puffy dome called an overshooting top appears.

Tornado formation begins with strong wind shear. Weak surface winds and stronger upper winds cause the air to start spinning horizontally. When this spinning air encounters an updraft, it gets pushed up and the rotation becomes vertical. This vertical column of spinning air may then lead to tornado formation.

A Tornado Appears

A funnel cloud

A mesocyclone starts out spinning slowly. But if conditions are just right, the rotation may speed up. The mesocyclone then stretches **vertically**. As it gets thinner, its spin increases. Eventually, the mesocyclone may reach the full depth of the storm, extending about nine miles (14 km) upward.

The bottom of the storm cloud may eventually bulge downward. This extended portion of the storm is called a wall cloud. It occurs near the **updraft**.

Meanwhile, the spin continues to increase. Then, a core of spinning air extends downward out of the cloud. The core continues to pull in more air. Inside the core, a funnel cloud may form and appear to grow downward. However, not all tornadoes have visible funnel clouds.

Finally, the funnel touches the ground in an explosion of dirt and debris. These materials spiral skyward. They

A tornado forming

quickly darken the funnel to form a solid-looking cone or column. Once the spinning air extends from cloud to ground, it is called a tornado.

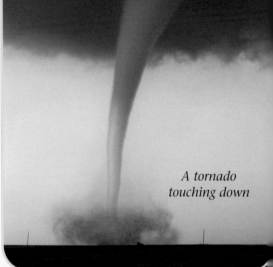

A tornado touching down

On the Ground

On the ground, a tornado can take many shapes. Some tornadoes look like ice-cream cones. Others look like slender fingers or ropes. Still others look like huge wedges or columns. A tornado can be smooth, bumpy, straight, or bent.

A tornado's shape and size can be misleading. Even thin, ropelike tornadoes can do major damage.

Tornadoes are not just shaped differently. They also come in many sizes. Average tornadoes are about 1,600 feet (500 m) wide. Others are raging monsters measuring more than one mile (2 km) across!

Whatever its size, an average tornado stays on the ground for about 15 minutes. Most tornadoes are weak and only last

When a tornado appears as wide as it is tall, it is described as a wedge.

two to three minutes. Still, all tornadoes leave trails of destruction wherever they go. This trail is called a path. After a tornado passes, scientists study its path. This helps them learn about the twister's size, strength, and life cycle.

Average tornadoes travel 27 to 29 miles per hour (43 to 47 km/h).

Wind Damage

A tornado's path can be a scene of incredible destruction. The worst twisters rip homes to shreds and toss around cars. They uproot trees, tear apart roads, and cut paths through crop fields.

All of this damage is caused by a tornado's high winds and debris. In the outer walls of the **vortex** core, air swirls at

speeds up to 280 to 360 miles per hour (450 to 575 km/h). These are the fastest winds that occur near Earth's surface.

Heavy boards, bricks, and even people can be sucked into the sky. The moving air smashes

Tornado winds can leave behind strange destruction. This house lost its roof, but everything stayed in place on the kitchen shelves!

It is important to be prepared for natural disasters such as tornadoes. Ask you parents to help you make a disaster supplies kit. Necessary items include food, drinking water, a flashlight, and batteries.

into solid objects and knocks them loose. This creates more debris, which the tornado moves upward and outward.

Large objects picked up by twisters do not usually travel far. Instead, they rise up a short distance. Then, the debris rains down from the tornado. This fast-moving material is deadly and adds to the damage a tornado causes.

Multiple Tornadoes

Tornadoes usually occur one at a time. But this is not always the case. Multiple tornadoes that come from the same **supercell** are called a tornado family. Tornado families may strike in a line. This forms a segmented damage path, like dashes along the ground.

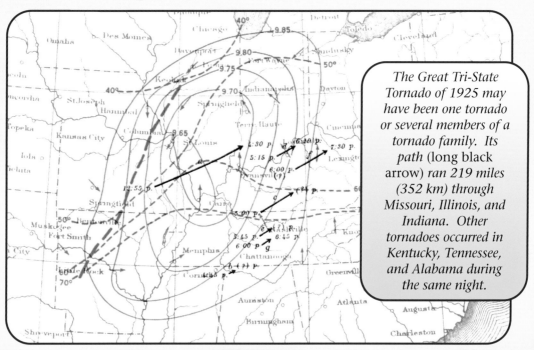

The Great Tri-State Tornado of 1925 may have been one tornado or several members of a tornado family. Its path (long black arrow) *ran 219 miles (352 km) through Missouri, Illinois, and Indiana. Other tornadoes occurred in Kentucky, Tennessee, and Alabama during the same night.*

Events called tornado **outbreaks** are even more extreme than tornado families. Tornado outbreaks get their start when several thunderstorms are part of the same large weather system. When conditions over a large area are right, tornado after tornado may drop from the clouds.

A small tornado outbreak consists of six to nine tornadoes. A medium outbreak has 10 to 19 tornadoes. Scientists classify 20 or more tornadoes as a large outbreak. Outbreaks are also organized by how large an area they affect. Local outbreaks occur in one state, while regional outbreaks include two to three. National tornado outbreaks occur in numerous states.

A satellite captured the path of this Maryland tornado, which extended for 24 miles (39 km).

Tornado Strength

Not all tornadoes are house-shredding monsters. Most twisters are weak or moderate in strength. Scientists use a system called the Enhanced Fujita (EF) Scale to describe these differences.

In 2007, an F5 tornado hit Greensburg, Kansas.

The EF-Scale ranks tornadoes from F0 to F5. F0 tornadoes have the weakest wind speeds. They range from 65 to 85 miles per hour (105 to 137 km/h). F5 tornadoes have wind speeds above 200 miles per hour (322 km/h). F1, F2, F3, and F4 storms fall between these extremes.

Scientists and their instruments cannot always get close enough to measure a tornado's winds. For this reason, they use ground damage to structures and **vegetation** as a guide.

For example, an F0 twister may damage chimneys and break tree branches. An F3 twister may overturn cars and tear the walls off houses. And, an F5 twister may destroy everything it touches.

Dr. Fujita

Dr. Tetsuya Theodore Fujita of the University of Chicago developed the Fujita Scale (F-Scale) in 1971. Like the EF-Scale, the F-Scale ranked all twisters from 0 to 5. But, many scientists felt the wind speeds in each category were too high. So, the new EF-Scale became official in February 2007.

The Enhanced Fujita Scale

SCALE	CLASS	WIND SPEED	DESCRIPTION
F0	weak	65–85 mph (105–137 km/h)	Gale
F1	weak	86–110 mph (138–177 km/h)	Moderate
F2	strong	111–135 mph (178–217 km/h)	Significant
F3	strong	136–165 mph (218–266 km/h)	Severe
F4	violent	166–200 mph (267–322 km/h)	Devastating
F5	violent	More than 200 mph (More than 322 km/h)	Incredible

Gathering Information

   The EF-Scale is useful. But, its rankings are based mostly on observation. Scientists must estimate wind speeds based on the damage a tornado caused. This means the measurements are not completely **accurate**.

   To get more precise information, scientists may use Doppler **radar**. A Doppler unit sends out radio waves. The waves bounce off particles in the tornado, such as raindrops and debris, and echo back. A computer then records the **frequency** of each returning wave. It uses this information to calculate the tornado's wind speeds.

   Doppler radar does not just measure tornadoes. It also warns scientists when twisters are forming. It does this by drawing computer images of **supercells**. Mesocyclones show up clearly on these pictures.

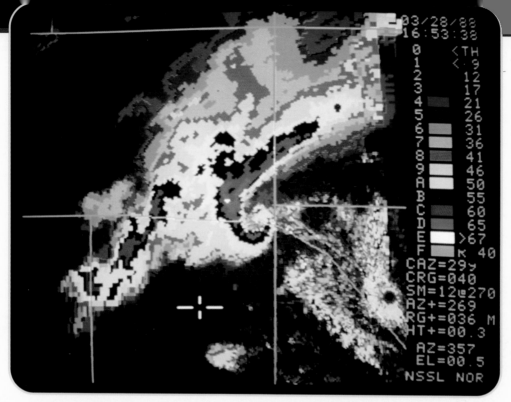

03/28/88
16:53:38
0   <TH
1   < 9
2   12
3   17
4   21
5   26
6   31
7   36
8   41
9   46
A   50
B   55
C   60
D   65
E   >67
F   κ 40
CAZ=299
CRG=040
SM=12ϑ270
AZ+=269
RG+=036 M
HT+=00.3
AZ=357
EL=00.5
NSSL NOR

On weather radar, a "hook echo" often shows the presence of a mesocyclone.
This indicates that a storm has started spinning, which could lead to a tornado.

When Doppler **radar** indicates a mesocyclone, scientists swing into action. Ground units or spotters also watch storms. When necessary, meteorologists and the National Weather Service issue statements to television and radio stations. The **media** then warns the public that conditions are right for a twister to occur.

Staying Safe

Everyone should know where to go to stay safe during a tornado. For this reason, schools and businesses often practice tornado drills. Homes in Tornado Alley often have built-in storm shelters. Residents flee to these underground rooms if a twister approaches.

Storm shelters are common in Tornado Alley. But, people everywhere can protect themselves from tornadoes. If a tornado is approaching, immediately seek shelter. An underground shelter is best, such as a storm cellar or a basement.

If there is no basement nearby, stay on the ground floor. Go to the innermost part of the building. Hide in a closet or another enclosed area, such as a bathroom. An area with sturdy walls and no windows is best. Cover yourself with blankets if you can. These barriers may shield you from flying debris.

If you are stuck outdoors, lie flat in a ditch. It is very unsafe to do this. But, a ditch is better than nothing if you cannot reach shelter.

Tornado drills help us remember what to do if a real tornado approaches. Go to a small, windowless area, such as an interior hallway. Then, crouch low with your hands protecting the back of your neck.

Chasing Twisters

Most people want to seek shelter when tornadoes approach. But others do just the opposite! They jump into their cars, trucks, and vans. Then, they head straight toward the twister. These people are called storm chasers, or "chasers" for short.

People have many reasons for following tornadoes. Some chasers are scientists. They want to get close enough to collect data. Other chasers are photographers or videographers. They spend their lives looking for the perfect shot. Still other chasers are thrill seekers. They just want to see a twister in action.

Storm chasers may have different interests. But they have something in common, too. They risk their lives to get close to tornadoes. Like people everywhere, they are fascinated by nature's most violent storms. Just make sure you leave the chasing to the professionals and seek shelter from twisters!

Chasers risk their lives to collect tornado data and photographs. This information furthers their understanding of these powerful storms.

Glossary

accurate - free of errors.

air mass - a large body of air containing nearly uniform temperature and humidity.

anvil - a heavy iron block used for shaping metal. Or, anything resembling an anvil in shape, such as a cumulonimbus cloud with a flat top.

dense - having a high mass per unit volume.

frequency - the number of waves, such as sound or radio waves, passing a fixed point each second.

horizontal - in a side-to-side direction.

media - a form or system of communication, information, or entertainment that includes television, radio, and newspapers.

outbreak - a sudden increase in activity or occurrence.

plain - a flat or rolling stretch of land without trees.

radar - a device that sends out and receives the reflections of radio waves, often used for detecting the location or speed of things.

supercell - a strong, long-lasting thunderstorm that has at least one rotating updraft and may cause tornadoes.

updraft - an upward movement of gas, such as air.

vegetation - plant life.

vertical - in an up-and-down position.

vortex - something resembling a whirlpool that draws things toward a central cavity.

Web Sites

To learn more about weather, visit ABDO Publishing Company on the World Wide Web at **www.abdopublishing.com**. Web sites about weather are featured on our Book Links page. These links are routinely monitored and updated to provide the most current information available.

Index